ARISE
SHINE

IMOGENE THOMAS RICE

Ufomadu Consulting & Publishing Group

United States   Europe   Africa

Copyright © 2023 by Imogene Thomas Rice

Published in the United States of America

No parts of this publication may be reproduced, stored in a retrieval system, or transmitted in a way by any means- electronic, mechanical, recording, or otherwise without the permission of the copyright holder, except as provided by USA law.

ISBN: 978-1-7331255-5-0

CONTENTS

Preface

About the Author

Acknowledgements

A Prepared Table for a Prepared People

The Prodigal Son

Sleeping with the Enemy

Will the Real Queen Stand Up

What Are You Asking For

Wounded Women in Relationships

Left Out but Not Forgotten

In the Desert but Not Alone

Rise and Shine Jesus is Alive

Spring Cleaning

The Football Church

Six Leading Ladies to Avoid

Keep On Keeping On

I am a Champion

Press On

All Things Work Together for the Good...

All Work and No Play

I Think I Can, I Know I Can

PREFACE

I thank God immensely for His grace, mercy, and many blessings He has generously showered on me. Without God I wouldn't have been able to do any of this. Writing a book is hard work but more rewarding than I could imagine.

Amen Pews: Arise & Shine was a title given to me when I was a teenager attending this little old wooden church house that sat on a hill where the people had real love for one another, and the saints would arise and fill the pews in thanks to God.

This book has made me laugh, cry, and reassess life. A spirit filled life is more than sitting on the pews on Sundays listening to the pastor and choir sing under the anointing of God. In addition, one can work outside by sharing the word and bringing someone to sit with you in the pew. The opportunity to share Jesus with others is very rewarding.

ABOUT THE AUTHOR

Imogene is a strong, confident, and intelligent woman who encourages others never to give up but continue to strive for greatness. She is a Christian woman who stands by what she speaks and teaches. Imogene has an unwavering love for God that is felt in the way she treats others. She is very compassionate and generous and always willing to share even if she has only two fish and five barley loaves. She speaks truth in words that bind lies. She stands with integrity and virtue.

ACKNOWLEDGEMENTS

Thanks to all of my readers for giving me the most important asset, your time. I assure you it will not be wasted. My desire is for you to be enriched every time you open the book.

I owe enormous debt of gratitude to Dr. and Mrs. Ufomadu at Ufomadu Consulting & Publishing Group for helping me develop and become this small town -country writer who never dreamed that I could.

Thanks to my special cheering team Patrick, Dallas R., C. Jones, A. Taylor, and C. Williams. You guys have supported and have done so much for me over the months while I was writing this book; I will always love you.

A PREPARED TABLE FOR A PREPARED PEOPLE

Sometimes when you go to dinner, you have no idea what you are going to be eating. Sometimes you like it, sometimes you make do with what's on the table. I remember one time my grandmother made a breakfast for my cousin and I that consisted of homemade biscuits, butter syrup, cured fat back meat and a glass of milk that we got from old Bessie in the barn. It was very delicious! "O taste and see that the Lord is good." Psalm 34:8. Yep, it was lip smacking good.

Be hopeful, for God is setting a table in your honor. "Eyes have not seen, ears have not heard, neither has it entered into the heart of men the good things God has in store for those who love Him."1st Corinthians 2:9.

God has placed a variety of foods on the table for us to enjoy, but you have to be prepared. The first item is forgiveness; oftentimes you hear people say, "I will forgive you, but I won't forget." Do yourself a favor and forget because God looked beyond our faults and continued to bless us.

The second dish on the table in a large white Victorian platter is Peace. You tore up the Deacon Board, causing trouble in the Choir, and gossiping about fellow Usher Board Members. Sister RudyRudi kept looking funny at sister Mae LeeLi because she was designated to prepare the Lord's supper for a month. You cannot hate brethren doing God's work and you cannot sow discord among brethren. Be the peacemaker among your group for, "Blessed are peacemakers for they shall be called the children of God. "Matthew 5:9.

The third dish on the table is a tough piece of meat. It is known as Patience. Sometimes when we are ready to eat the meal it is not ready, and we look for snacks as a substitute and when the dinner is finally served, we are already filled with junk. Have you noticed people who are always in a hurry with no place to go? They want a blessing with their name on it but are not willing to wait until the roast is ready. We all sometimes struggle with waiting on the Lord. The point here is that lack of patience can cause us to miss our blessing. Always remember, "They that wait upon the LORD shall renew their strength; they shall mount up with wings as eagles; they shall run, and not be weary; and they shall walk, and not faint." Isaiah 40:31

The fourth dish has to be cooked overnight in the oven at 400 degrees. Once the cooking process is completed the roast has to sit in the oven for at least 6 hours before serving, it is known as Long Suffering. To sit and eat this meal, one has to go through difficult times; so oftentimes, we as saints of God cannot endure challenges as little as people speaking negatively of us. When people say something we disagree with, the best thing to do is to endure instead jumping up and down, causing unnecessary fracas. We have to learn "To endure hardship as a good soldier of Jesus Christ." 2nd Timothy 2:3.

Well, we are about to clean up the chicken with LOVE which is also kind. Sometimes when we dine out with friends, they pick up the tab. According to John 3:16, we were not able to pay our debt, so God sent His only son to pay our bill. Our sins were too great for any man to pay. When all was paid, He bowed His head and cried it is finished. All was done in LOVE.

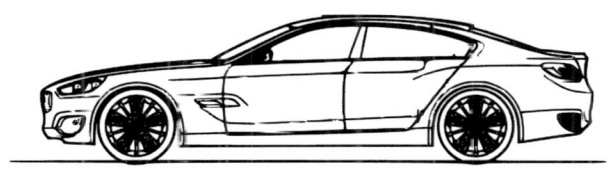

THE PRODIGAL SON

We know the story all too well. It's retold countless times during church homecoming and family get-togethers. There was a man who had two sons. One day the younger son came to his father and asked for his share of the inheritance. The father granted the son's request without question. After receiving his inheritance, the son packed his bags and placed them in his Red 2 door Chevy Camaro V8 455 Horsepower and headed down that long dusty road as his father looked into the dust with sadness in his heart. His mother stood inside this old wooden framed house looking out of the east window with tears in her eyes and a prayer on her lips, as her son headed in the wrong direction.

At the end of this long dusty road the son had a choice, he could continue or turn back. But, this young man chose to continue on his journey where the streetlight shined brighter than the old pole light in his parent's front yard. His pockets were filled with cash, and he was excited about being on his own.

After a few days of living in a 4-bedroom apartment with his girlfriend, partying every night with his new buddies, drinking champagne, wine, eating steaks and caviar, his pockets became empty within a short period of time. He had no money for food, no place to lay his head, and no place to call home.

When this young man came to himself, he said "Well, I guess I better get on back home and ask for forgiveness." Early one Sunday morning just before the sun rose above the trees the father came out and looked down that long dusty road and saw a shadow of a man coming toward him with a slight limp and a brown paper bag in his hand. The father recognized his son from afar and yelled, "Junior! Hey y'all, here comes my son!"

    Mother ran out onto that old wooden porch with tears of joy thanking God for keeping her son safe. This young man had sold his car, his luggage, and also sold his pride.

The son began to ask the family for forgiveness. The father, having much compassion and love for his son said, "go in the house and get cleaned up for we are going to have a get together in your honor."

    We as Christians have walked away from God like the prodigal son. We have forgotten that old magnolia tree that covered the park's bench in which we would sit and meditated on the goodness of God. Misplaced that old Gospel Pearl song book that made our feet go tap- tap; closed the window blinds and locked up the prayer room. God is waiting with open arms to restore us if we would confess our sins. He would wash us up, put a robe of righteousness on us, and a ring on our finger and celebrate with exceeding great joy.

SLEEPING WITH THE ENEMY

Judges 13:1-5

Samson went down to Timnah and became friends with this beautiful woman, and she was talking his language. They began holding hands and looking into each other's eyes until they desired to move forward to the bedroom. Samson was a playboy who loved women. The enemy will learn your strength and weakness to destroy life. Samson disobeyed God and his parents. He grew up quickly and became his own man with his own life instructions. This was the beginning of his downfall. Oftentimes children become displeased with parents when they begin to correct them about life and its pitfalls.

Samson went down to Gaza and there he encountered failure. He met Delilah; he made no attempt to marry her; he just wanted sex in the back room. You cannot play with fire and not get burned. Samson used his gift for personal gain. It's not written where he raised up an army or called a meeting with the brothers; sex and women was at the top of his agenda like so many men today called by God. The enemy will strip you down to shame; you can't praise or worship God. If you have no desire to pray, Spiritual strength is gone in a ceremony, you have to return to that you lost! Yes! Return to that you lost.

WILL THE REAL QUEEN STAND UP?

Esther I

Queen Vashti was a beautiful woman. She had character, class, respect, and wisdom. At King Ahasuerus' convention he wanted the men to see his crown jewel. He wanted to brag to the fellows about this good looking woman of his. King Ahasuerus didn't love the queen as much as he pretended. He wanted to parade her in the presence of his drunk buddies. Well, you know the old saying, "A drunk always speaks his mind."

I imagine that at Queen Vashti's party she was teaching the young women how to be a keeper of home (Titus 2:3-5) and how to preserve their bodies until marriage, and in doing so, they would receive the title of a Queen along with rubies, silver, gold, and that Bentley.

We as African American Queens deserve respect and should demand it. We are the mothers of the African American male and the pillar of the family. Oftentimes, we as women lower our standards and become satisfied with nothing. At the end of the day, we have to rub our own feet, run our own bath water, and turn back our own bed sheets. A Queen looks for love and security in a relationship, not a trick.

After King Ahasuerus had sobered up and had been defeated in Greece, his ego was low, and he felt sorry for listening to his buddies telling him what he should do about his Queen. Sometimes we allow people to dictate our relationship and when it is no longer in operation, we find ourselves saying, I wish, I should have, I could have. Stop receiving ungodly advice from people with no wisdom. There is no sunshine when she is gone.

Will the Real Queen Stand UP?

WHAT ARE YOU ASKING FOR?

AGAIN, WHAT ARE YOU ASKING FOR?

Peter and John were on their way to church around 3 o'clock to pray when a man with a medical condition got their attention. This man was lame from his mother's womb. Everywhere he went someone had to carry him. People dropped him off every day at the church gate for years to beg for money. I asked myself why not drop him off at the club, because there are more people there than at the church? This man was probably begging for his friends; he couldn't go to buy groceries, pay a bill, or buy personal items. His buddies were using him and the church. They left him on the emergency steps and went back home. This man possibly had lost hope in himself and felt like an outcast.

Peter and John stopped when they heard this pitiful voice begging. They had compassion for their brother and commanded him to get up and walk in the name of Jesus. Peter pulled him up by his right hand and immediately the man felt something happening that he never felt before. Blood started running warm in his veins; he felt a tingling that signaled he could support his own weight. This brother came into the church with a song on his lips "Since Jesus came into my heart." Jesus is our HOPE OF GLORY!

WOUNDED WOMEN IN RELATIONSHIPS

Psalm 107

We as women have so many wounds and scars that are not healed; we place a band-aid over it and keep moving. So many of us are beaten up, torn up, and messed up in relationships that were not ordained by God, now we have almost lost our anointing and our minds are on the border line of Help Me Please and We Cannot Encourage Ourselves in the Lord. Isaiah 40:31 "They that wait upon the Lord shall renew their strength."

So many of us didn't wait for God to send Boaz, instead we settled for his second cousin who was downright no good and called it a blessing from God.

We as wounded women need to love ourselves and know what we bring to the table. You are a child of God so stand up straight and tell June Bug and Bay Brother that it's not tonight and he should get his bags and go. Be careful who enters into your physical and spiritual house.

I heard Rev. E. Jackson from Ohio tell the young ladies back in those days who were married, "Baby if you make your bed hard you got to lay in it." They didn't believe in separation or divorce. My friend, it's okay to change your bed sheets and freshen up your bed. Lying in that bed in the same position can cause bed sores. It's a new day. Get up!!!

LEFT OUT BUT NOT FORGOTTEN

John 4:3-11

Sometimes we forget about our families, friends, and yes, our spouse. I realized while reading John 4:3-11 that Jesus had to go through Samaritan, because His daughter was there feeling left out and perhaps embarrassed, because of her low status and reputation.

This Samaritan woman went to the well at the hottest hour of the day to draw water, because she wanted to avoid the Sunday or going to meet the saints, who talked about everybody and everything. The church had written this woman off, took her name off the church roll book and placed it on the street signs for easy reading. No one can hurt you like church folks. They can cut you down to the white meat, where only the Great Physician can heal.

Jesus had to go through Samaritan and the woman had to be at the well. It's a blessing to be in the right place at the right time to hear a word from the Lord. Jesus was concerned about His daughter. We don't know her name or what happened to those five husbands she had or why they left her, but this woman had more to give than most people realized. She approached the well with the water pots on her shoulders, which told me she was under pressure.

The Sunday go to meet saints didn't visit her and surely, they were not praying for her. This woman was left out but not forgotten. She needed a word of hope. When she came in contact with Jesus, He didn't insult her nor did He judge her, but He pulled the mask off her face. He exposed her privately. So, oftentimes as Christians we feel that we are covered up really good from our sins, but God will expose us in His timing.

This Samaritan woman stood before Jesus embarrassed, her secrets had been revealed and now she had to face the Master and confess her sins. Once my sister confessed, Satan could no longer hold her in bondage.

This woman did not understand everything Jesus was saying to her, but she knew He did not try to take advantage of her. After their conversation, this woman went up town. It didn't matter who saw her or what they were saying behind her back. My sister's concern was "come see a man who told me everything I had ever done." She didn't tell the people what Jesus said to her. Some things should be your own best kept secret. This Samaritan woman dropped her water pots and became a new person, for old things have passed away behold all things have become new. 2 Corinthians 5:17.

There comes a time in life when you cannot send an individual; you must go yourself because the task is too important for mistakes. Jesus needed to speak directly to the Samaritan woman face to face. He wanted to assure her that He was the one she had been looking for. Sometimes we look for love in all the wrong places and from the wrong people.

Jesus gave my sister a full time job as an "Evangelist Samaritan." She didn't have to fill out an application, submit a resume or wait to be called for an interview. So, oftentimes we miss our assignment because we are not willing to drop our pots. God wants to give you a job, are you ready for the interview?

IN THE DESERT BUT NOT ALONE

Genesis 16: 1-8

When we speak of the desert, things come to mind such as a dry deserted place where lizards, scorpions, and cactus live. These things are somewhat dangerous to the touch. Genesis 16:1-8 talks about Hagar, her son, Abram, and Sarai. Hagar's name means Light. She was sold and purchased by Abram for his wife's servant. Hagar and Sarai had a good relationship until Sari wanted Hagar to become a surrogate mother. Sari was like so many of us who are not willing to wait on the Lord; therefore, we take matters into our own hands and cause a mess. Sari mistreated Hagar just because she had authority. God never desired for us to be abused or victimized. No matter what we are going through, God is there alongside of us. Hagar said, "He is a God who seeth." Nothing is hidden from His eyes. Hagar was placed in a situation that did not honor God, yet He took care of her. He looked upon her as a good mother. God understood Hagar's pain; He gave her the opportunity to express her true feelings in this dry place. So, oftentimes you hear church leaders say, "give God some praise." The first thing we do is clap our hands, but God wants to hear our words, so open up your mouth and say something.

Hagar was in this dry place with no one to call on for support, but God had a master plan for her and her son according to Romans 8:28. "All things work together for the good of those who love the Lord and according to His purpose."

How can you identify an individual in a dry place? Well, praying with no change; laying of hands but no healing; prophesying but nothing coming to pass; outreach ministry, but no drawing power; preaching but nobody is being saved. Dry place.

God called Hagar by her name, and it gave her hope and strength to hold on and hold out. No one came to the desert to check on her and her son. She was feeling the misery of her past and not sure about her future. Sometimes life makes you feel dry and lonely, but help is always present. People may use you as a stepping stone to the top, but stay strong my sister. Hang in there my brother, God seeth.

RISE AND SHINE, JESUS IS ALIVE

Revelation 1:18

Jesus' death allowed us to be pardoned from our sins and His resurrection is proof that the payment was accepted. Now we can face tomorrow with hope.

The enemy counted you out and said you would not make it. As far as they were concerned, you no longer matter- they had your funeral and read your obituary aloud. Amazingly, Jesus announced that He was going to lay down His life and rise with all power in His hands. Some people didn't believe, but when the enemy saw you standing in the congregation of the saints they were overwhelmed because they thought it was over.

Early one morning Peter and John heard from Mary Magdalene that the body of Jesus had been taken. He is no longer in the tomb. Jesus is alive forever.

Rise and Shine Jesus is Alive!

Spring Cleaning

Isaiah 54:17

This is an activity that all household members can participate in. We can spend hours cleaning the windows after the rain, the snow, the dust, and grime build up over the fall and winter months. This build up causes our windows to become dim making it hard to see clearly. During this spring cleaning we realize that some things need to be thrown away and some need to be burned up.

This household cleaning is only temporary, but the spiritual cleaning will last a lifetime according to Psalm 51:10. The first thing we need to throw away is Pride; this will cause suffering and negative behavior. Pride needs to be replaced with Humility. "God resists the proud, but gives grace to the humble." James 4:6. The second is Anger; some of us get angry at the drop of a pin and fly off in a minute. We need to burn anger and replace it with Self-Control. "An angry man stirs up strife and a furious man abounds in transgression." Proverb 29:22.

Thirdly, we need to get rid of Unbelief and substitute it with Faith. John 3:16. Finally, here comes Revenge. Let's get rid of these old bags, such as Unforgiveness and Bitterness. This is like an old footlocker in the attic you want to keep. We have to release people and replace Revenge with Forgiveness.

No one said it would be easy because sometimes that footlocker is really heavy.

    Let's clean out Complaining because some of us complain and argue about nothing. We cause division in the church, community, workplace and in the family. Nobody is right but me, myself, and I. We need to burn up that Self-Righteous Spirit and replace it with Praise. "Do all things without complaining." Philippians 2:14."

    We are about to take the garbage bags to the dump and throw away Gossip and replace it with Encouragement. Without wood a fire goes out; just like without gossip a quarrel dies. We need to build each other in love. Proverb 26:20 puts it this way, "where no wood is, there the fire goeth out: so, where there is no talebearer, the strife ceaseth. As coals are to hot embers, and wood to fire, so is a contentious man to kindle strife."

THE FOOTBALL CHURCH

There are 10 plays on this team; you have the Quarterback Sneak, Draw Play, Halftime, Benchwarmer, Backfield-in-Motion, Staying-in-Pocket, Two Minute Warning, End Run, Flex Defense, and the Blitz.

Let's kick off with the Quarterback Sneak, here is where church members quietly leave when invited to church. They feel there is no need to stay around, because they are filled with the Holy Spirit and Fire Baptized. There is nothing that needs to be placed on the altar, therefore, this part of the service is of no importance to them.

Now, the Draw Play. Here we get ready to recite our ABC'S. The Church Ushers begin to pass out the church bulletin before worship with the order of service, announcements, and upcoming events. During service adults pretend to be taking notes, but they are drawing and playing while the children are writing on everything except themselves. Once confronted you leave the church reciting your ABC's.

Halftime is the period between Sunday School and Worship when many choose to make a run to Mickey D's for breakfast. Sunday School is the beginning of worship in teaching. Now you are full and ready for a nap pretending to hear the word of the Lord.

Benchwarmer: these are the fault finding folks always talking about something and someone. They don't sing, pray, or give.

Backfield-in-Motion: here the bathroom is on call. "Well, I had to take my medicine this morning; therefore, I have to go, you know." On your way back to service you stop by the water fountain for a sip of water and head back into the bathroom for relaxation and wait to be joined by other members.

Staying-in-the-Pocket in this case is what happens to most money that should be given to the church for the up building of the Lord's house, but instead it's staying in the pocket.

The Two Minute Warning is when you realize the sermon is almost over and you begin to gather up the children and other belongings ready to head to the nearest exit.

End Run, Touchdown, Ready-Set-Go is leaving quickly without speaking to anyone.

Flex Defense are the ones who allow absolutely nothing said by the pastor to affect them. They feel the sermon was fitting for others.

Then, there's the Blitz. Here, we are rushing to the restaurant for 2 sides, a piece of meat, a slice of pie and a glass of sweet tea. Just finished eating the bread of life and still hungry for more eating, calling it socialization.

SIX LEADING LADIES TO AVOID

If you want to be successful in ministry, avoid these six leading ladies. This first lady is known as the Diva. Ministry is all about her; she is the star of the show and is known for her demands. Someone has to carry her bible, water bottle, purse, and the cell phone. No one should carry your weapons or purse, and not even your water bottle; saint's still practice witchcraft in the church and your cell phone is not as important as the Word of God. When this Diva is asked to preach the word of Lord at your Women's Conference, you learn quickly that she is high priced. She requires the high priced hotels, fancy riding car, and over half of the offering in which she collected by running a church auction. This Diva would stop studying the bible and focus on her conference outfits. She loves a grand entrance, coming in late and leaving without spending time in prayer with the needy.

This second woman is a Control Freak. She rules with an iron fist and leaves wounded people behind. You can't tell her nothing, she knows it all. This woman never learned that a good follower makes a good leader.

The Flirt is the third woman to avoid at all costs. She has a problem with dress code, men's code; you name it. This woman walks to the podium wearing a dress revealing all the body parts. Some of the men start looking at the floor because Peter is about to jump out of the gate. There is a professional dress code for women in ministry. Godly women should be role models for other women, not a sex weapon. They do not have to wear flannel dresses on the floor and the hair in a bun to be modest. There is nothing wrong with looking like a million bucks. This flirting woman hangs around with men alone in the church office and even counsels them alone. She forgot to read Romans 14:16 "Don't let your good be spoken of."

The Fake is another woman we need to avoid. We need leaders who understand the gift of the Holy Spirit and realize that no one who steps out into the supernatural is going to be correct 100% of the time. "We prophesy in part" 1 Corinthians 13:9-12. This woman will always say "I heard from the Lord". It's sad to have fake people on the pews, but when they are elevated to leadership positions you encounter problems. This woman suffers from depression.

The Feminist is another one of these women we need to stay far away from. She may be gifted but listen closely to her speaking for the reason that she has not forgiven the men who hurt her in the past. This woman has many unsolved issues and brings them to the church house. This lady has experienced at least one failed marriage and not one healthy relationship. She needs a lot of counseling before entering another relationship or any church position.

Well, here comes the Victim, she is the most pitiful of all. She is guaranteed to make you feel sorry for her. She might use a full box of Kleenex for you to understand her pain. She lacks leadership skills and believes everybody is against her, including family. Her ministry is always in turmoil. This lady wants a small remnant of people in her group who have similar emotional baggage.

All of these negative women are in the church today. I am looking to see an army of Real Gifted Trained Women who will serve as Real Pastors, Missionaries, Evangelists, CEO's, and Leaders who will rightly share the Word of Truth.

Instead of Divas, we need real women who are willing to serve even if they do not receive public recognition. Instead of a Control Freak, we need leaders who will wash the feet of others and push them to greatness. Instead of Flirts, we need mature women and dignified mothers of faith who have been crucified. Rather than the Fake women who are tossed around by every wind that comes along, we need biblical truth.

Rather than the Feminists, we need women who have resolved their issues with men. Rather than a Victim, we need women in ministry who are emotionally healed and not crazy.

If you are called to leadership, God will guide the preparation process and He will bring mentors and positive role models to encourage you. Allow the Holy Spirit to shape your character. God doesn't choose those who are qualified, He qualifies those He calls to get the job done.

Be Strong!

KEEP ON KEEPING ON

2 Corinthians 4:6-8

I was inspired by God years ago to write this amazing book. To encourage hurting women, but not limited to women. We as women hurt in so many ways, such as family, relationship, friendship, and, oh yes, church. All of this can bring depression and even suicide attempts. Many times, life situations happen that cause us to feel beaten and broken. Sometimes we feel beyond repair, but, if you put all things in the Hands of God through prayer and supplication you can and will overcome every battle. I am reminded of James Langston Hughes, *Mother to Son*. "Life for me ain't been no crystal stair, it had tacks in it, And splinter's, And board torn up, And place with no carpet on the floor.... Bare. But all the time, I've been a climbin' on, And reachin' landin's, And turnin' corners, And sometime goin' in the dark Where there ain't been no light."

A mother's words of encouragement can be the foundation for which greatness is built. You are indeed a phenomenal woman. Lift your chin from your chest, hold your head up, never give up, pick yourself up, brush yourself off, push toward, and don't fall.

I've fallen so many times already, but hope and faith kept me rising, "Now unto Him who is able to keep you from falling, and to present you faultless before the presence of His glory with exceeding joy." (Jude 1:24)

Woman, let me remind you again to keep your head up because if it's down you won't be able to see the blessings God has placed in your life. I know life is tough, but God cares about you! He wants you to live gracefully, He will help you with all your hardships and trials. In the end you will rise up with a testimony waiting to be told. No matter what the situation is, your blessing always outweighs the disappointments.

Go back to high school and get that diploma, get that college degree, start your own business, become the CEO, or director of that up and coming business that God has planted in you. Build yourself to be a woman that, when your son or daughter sees you, they will know you are a woman who worked for her goals. Set an example. Never underestimate what you can do if you've never tried. You're smart enough, good enough, beautiful enough and strong enough. Yesterday is gone, today is warming up and the future is calling your name. Will you answer the call? Stop looking back on mistakes, learn from them and move on, one foot in front of the other. It's hard to learn from mistakes without consequences. Stay strong, be happy and make them wonder how you are still smiling. Share your smile, clap for a winner, help lift someone who has fallen, celebrate with others and the same will be shown to you when it's your turn to be celebrated.

I AM A CHAMPION

Romans 8:31-38

Life has many chapters, what are we going to write today? You may be at a bad chapter, but it doesn't mean it's the end of the book; turn the page, you have three choices, give up, give in, or give it all you've got. Every champion was once a contender who refused to give up. Champions believe in themselves when no one else does. Winning is about staying on your feet. You're capable of amazing things. Never let anyone discourage your spirit. Never stop praying, pray with a clean heart, clean hands and with faith that all things will come together in God's timing. It doesn't matter how fast or slow you move toward your goal as long as you get there. Yes, you may mess up but do not sit there and let it ruin your dreams. Get up, no matter how much it hurts. Don't stop when you are hurting or tired; stop when you have finished the task.

I have failed many times and still kept going. I have learned the more I fail, the more I learn. You have a choice; you can throw in the towel or you can use it to wipe the sweat from your face. It's your choice. Don't be afraid to walk into greatness. God sees you when you don't see Him working on your behalf. Struggles are required in life in order to survive. Start where you are, use what you have and do what you can. You are never sent a reward for no reason; you have to earn it. Stop spending your time on people that do not care about you, start spending time to better yourself. If you give up at the first sign of a struggle, you are not ready to be successful.

PRESS ON

Matthew 19:26

Hello there, lift your head up. What's the matter with you? Be the woman or man you want to be. Go for it and expect it to come to pass. No matter the disappointments, God is blessing in amazing ways. See your blessing and dream big. But, let me serve you notice, if your dream doesn't come to pass right away don't get depressed and most of all don't lose hope. When God closes one door, He opens another. Everything you need to be successful is inside of you. The first step to success is not doing something great, but appreciating and acknowledging great things that other people do. Stay away from people who try to belittle your dreams.

Small people will do that, but great people will make you feel that you can. You can't always wait for the perfect time. Sometimes you must leap. Life is all about risk and it requires you to leap. Don't be that person who looks back and wonders what they could've or would've. Yes, you are going to make mistakes. You're going to go about something the wrong way, but what do we do? Hit the reset button and press on. You are the director of your own life. Stop asking for permission. Don't let people take you to a dead end. The greatest battle is not physical, but psychological. Great things never come from your comfort zone. Your life is a book; make it a bestseller. Work until your signature becomes your autograph. Every successful person has a painful story and a beautiful ending.

My friend, you're beautiful, handsome, talented, amazing, and the best. To be a champion you must believe you are the best. Even if you are not, pretend you are and watch God work. God didn't create us to be average, He didn't make us to barely get by. We were created to excel. Encourage yourself, believe in yourself, love yourself and push yourself above the negativity of others. Do not let them touch you with their nasty hands. You are a warrior! Warriors don't give up and they don't back down. David had to encourage himself. (1 Samuel 30:6) Your words carry amazing power. (Proverb 18:21)

Make a list of your weaknesses and work on them one by one. There is no cutting corners or shortcuts in life. Remember, true greatness does not have to be announced. Becoming great has a lot to do with being humble.

Keep in mind, if you can't fly then run. If you can't run, then walk. If you can't walk, then crawl. Whatever you decide, keep pressing on. God doesn't make mistakes, but He does miracles.

ALL THINGS WORK TOGETHER FOR THE GOOD OF THOSE WHO LOVE GOD

Romans 8:28

Before you begin a new day, know exactly where you are headed. In life there are criers, triers, and liars. Which one are you? If you look deep within yourself, you'll probably find an old dream that has been tarnished from neglect; get it out and shine it up. If you believe deep within you that you deserve to have beautiful things, manifest them into reality. Some people spend their entire lives waiting patiently for "someday". You may be thirty, forty, or eighty years old; never throw away your dream. It is never too late to get an education in almost anything. The internet and libraries are full of books on every subject. There are night classes, adult education courses, private instructors, and much more waiting on you. Visualize and see your goal. Too many of us are not living our dreams, but living our fears. Ten years from now you will be more disappointed by the things you didn't do than by the ones you did. It's not about getting knocked down, it's about whether you get up or lay there. If you fall on your face, keep moving. Dreams don't work unless you make them work. If you think down will go down, if you think up you will go in that direction. "If you have faith in the size of a mustard seed nothing is impossible." Luke 17:6.

ALL WORK AND NO PLAY

Rise and shine! What are you waiting for? It's a new day. Let's go toward our goal; don't lay there dreaming. Get on your feet, get dressed, and put on your shoes. No matter how you feel, you can't have a million dollar dream with a minimum work ethic.

Create high standards for yourself, expect the best, and work hard. You will encounter setbacks and occasional failures, but don't stop. The sky is the limit if you are for real. I feel anyone can do anything they set their mind to; it just depends on how bad you want it. When they say you can't, prove them wrong by giving 100% plus, and an additional 100% of hard work. Remember to trust in the Lord with all your heart, and do not lean on your own understanding. In all your ways acknowledge Him and He will direct your path. Proverbs 3:5-6.

If opportunity is knocking at your door, don't just stand there and listen or hide pretending you're not there, looking through the peephole. Open the door and grasp the opportunity before it goes to the next person's door.

If you don't take the time to sharpen your axe, you'll spend your life hacking at missed opportunities. Life is like a wheelbarrow; nothing will happen until you start pushing. I have been through life's joy and pain, sunshine and rain, sadness, and gladness, but these things are what makes life complete for me to have a testimony to tell. Difficult roads sometimes lead to beautiful destinations. Close the doors on the past and open the doors to the future. Take a deep breath, step on through, and start a new chapter of life.

Success doesn't happen overnight. Keep your eyes on the prize and don't look back. Surround yourself with people who see greatness in you even when you don't see it yourself. Don't just sit there wishing. Stand on your feet.

Well, I hope I've encouraged you to visualize and achieve.

I THINK I CAN, I KNOW I CAN

Isaiah 41:10

"So do not fear, for I am with you; do not be dismayed, for I am your God. I will strengthen you and help you; I will uphold you with my righteous hand." Isaiah 41:10. Just a reminder to let you know that in order to be successful you have to use each day as an opportunity to improve and bring yourself closer to your goals. Push yourself, dream it, wish it, and do it.

It's going to be hard, but hard doesn't mean impossible. People who wonder if the glass is half full miss the point. The glass is refillable. Keep your eyes on the prize and your feet on the ground. Nothing will work unless you do. In the face of difficulty lies opportunity.

We are our sisters' and brothers' keepers. Oftentimes I am reminded of the Good Samaritan. (Luke 10:29-37) The Priest and a Levite both passed by this "broken man" they looked upon him but refused to offer him a hand up. The Samaritan had compassion for this brother.

Hebrew 13:2 tells us to be aware of how we, as Christians, treat one another. A large percent of church pews are empty today; the flocks are scattered and the few that remain are spiritually frail; they're too weak to say Amen!

NOTES

NOTES

References

https:// bing.com/images

https://canva.com

https://clipartpanda.com

Hughes, Langston (1922). *Mother to Son.* https://poetryfoundation.org

https://www.istockphoto.com

https://www.istockphoto.com/illustrations/fine-dining-table-setting-clip-art

Kanvictory, Homeless Man Begging for Money, Canva.com.<https://www.canva.com/>

King James Bible (2017). King James Bible

https://www.kingjamesbibleonline.org

Pixabay.com

Pixabay, Sports Car Illustration, Canva.com.<https://www.canva.com/>

Pixabay (GDJ), Illustration of a Crown, Canva.com.<https://www.canva.com/>

Vasile-saptefrati, Be Strong, Canva.com, <https://www.canva.com/>

Vintage Illustrations, The Ascension of Jesus at the Mount of Olives, Canva.com. <https://www.canva.com/>

www.ingramcontent.com/pod-product-compliance
Lightning Source LLC
Chambersburg PA
CBRC092058200426
43209CB00067B/1869